MIX
Papier aus verantwortungsvollen Quellen
Paper from responsible sources
FSC® C105338

Priyanka Nandal

Malware Detection

Anchor Academic
Publishing

Nandal, Priyanka: Malware Detection, Hamburg, Anchor Academic Publishing 2017

Buch-ISBN: 978-3-96067-208-1
PDF-eBook-ISBN: 978-3-96067-708-6
Druck/Herstellung: Anchor Academic Publishing, Hamburg, 2017

Bibliografische Information der Deutschen Nationalbibliothek:
Die Deutsche Nationalbibliothek verzeichnet diese Publikation in der Deutschen Nationalbibliografie; detaillierte bibliografische Daten sind im Internet über http://dnb.d-nb.de abrufbar.

Bibliographical Information of the German National Library:
The German National Library lists this publication in the German National Bibliography. Detailed bibliographic data can be found at: http://dnb.d-nb.de

All rights reserved. This publication may not be reproduced, stored in a retrieval system or transmitted, in any form or by any means, electronic, mechanical, photocopying, recording or otherwise, without the prior permission of the publishers.

Das Werk einschließlich aller seiner Teile ist urheberrechtlich geschützt. Jede Verwertung außerhalb der Grenzen des Urheberrechtsgesetzes ist ohne Zustimmung des Verlages unzulässig und strafbar. Dies gilt insbesondere für Vervielfältigungen, Übersetzungen, Mikroverfilmungen und die Einspeicherung und Bearbeitung in elektronischen Systemen.

Die Wiedergabe von Gebrauchsnamen, Handelsnamen, Warenbezeichnungen usw. in diesem Werk berechtigt auch ohne besondere Kennzeichnung nicht zu der Annahme, dass solche Namen im Sinne der Warenzeichen- und Markenschutz-Gesetzgebung als frei zu betrachten wären und daher von jedermann benutzt werden dürften.

Die Informationen in diesem Werk wurden mit Sorgfalt erarbeitet. Dennoch können Fehler nicht vollständig ausgeschlossen werden und die Diplomica Verlag GmbH, die Autoren oder Übersetzer übernehmen keine juristische Verantwortung oder irgendeine Haftung für evtl. verbliebene fehlerhafte Angaben und deren Folgen.

Alle Rechte vorbehalten

© Anchor Academic Publishing, Imprint der Diplomica Verlag GmbH
Hermannstal 119k, 22119 Hamburg
http://www.diplomica-verlag.de, Hamburg 2017
Printed in Germany

TABLE OF CONTENTS

Chapter 1: Introduction..6-36

    1.1 Types of Malware...8

        1.1.1 Virus..9

            1.1.1.1 Virus Classification by Target....................................9

            1.1.1.2 Virus Classification by Self Protection Strategy......10

        1.1.2 Worm..11

            1.1.2.1 Activation...11

            1.1.2.2 Payload...12

            1.1.2.3 Target Discovery..12

            1.1.2.4 Propagation...13

        1.1.3 Trojans..14

            1.1.3.1 How Trojans work 15

            1.1.3.2 Trojans Types...16

        1.1.4 Adware...18

        1.1.5 Spyware..18

        1.1.6 Rootkit..19

        1.1.7 Backdoor..19

        1.1.8 Keylogger...19

        1.1.9 Ransomware...19

        1.1.10 Remote Administration Tools..19

        1.1.11 Botnet...20

1.1.12 Scareware..20

1.2 Malware Classification Tree...21

1.3 Classification Methods..22

    1.3.1 Supervised Methods..22

        1.3.1.1 Naive Bayes Classifier..22

        1.3.1.2 J48 Decision Trees..23

        1.3.1.3 Support Vector Machines..24

        1.3.1.4 K-nearest neighbors...26

        1.3.1.5 N-grams..27

    1.3.2 Unsupervised Methods...29

        1.3.2.1 K-means clustering algorithm..29

1.4 Difference between K-nearest neighbor and K-means clustering algorithm.............30

1.5 Malware Detection Techniques..31

    1.5.1 Signature Based Detection..31

    1.5.2 Anomaly Based Detection..32

    1.5.3 Heuristic Analysis or Pro-Active Defense..32

        1.5.3.1 Hidden Markov Model Based Detection..32

    1.5.4 Genetic Signature Detection...33

1.6 Malware Detection Tools...34

    1.6.1 Microsoft Process Explorer..34

    1.6.2 Trend Micro's HijackThis..34

    1.6.3 Kaspersky's GetSystemInfo...34

  1.6.4 Microsoft Baseline Security Analyzer..35

  1.6.5 Secunia inspection scanners..35

  1.6.6 Antivirus Programs..35

  1.6.7 Microsoft's Malicious Software Removal Tool...35

  1.6.8 SUPER Antispyware...36

  1.6.9 Malware byte's Anti-Malware...36

  1.6.10 GMER..36

Chapter 2: Literature Survey...37-50

 2.1 Data Mining...37

  2.1.1 Dynamic Misuse Detection 37

  2.1.2 Dynamic Hybrid Detection 38

  2.1.3 Static Anomaly Detection 39

  2.1.4 Static Hybrid Detection..39

  2.1.5 Static Misuse Detection..41

 2.2 Machine Learning...42

 2.3 Cloud Computing..47

 2.4 Android Malware Detection...49

Chapter 3: Implementation..51-58

 3.1 Problem Description...51

 3.2 System Requirements 51

 3.3 Datasets Used..52

 3.4 Process Outline..53

3.4.1 Sandbox Configuration..53

3.4.2 Feature extraction and selection...53

3.4.3 Application of classification methods..55

3.5 Results and Discussion...57

Chapter 4: Conclusion and Future work...59

4.1 Conclusion...59

4.2 Future Work...59

References..60-66

LIST OF FIGURES

Figure 1: No. of Malware Specification 8

Figure 2: Malware Classification Tree 21

Figure 3: SVM Scheme 25

Figure 4: KNN Scheme 26

Figure 5: Screenshot of .bytes file 54

Figure 6: Screenshot of .asm file 54

Figure 7: Screenshot of prediction file 57

CHAPTER 1
INTRODUCTION

Computer security, also known as cyber security or IT security is the protection of computer systems from the theft or damage to their hardware, software or information, as well as from disruption or misdirection of the services they provide. The security controls are used to provide confidentiality, integrity, and availability of data, software, hardware, and firmware of computer systems. To secure a computer system, it is important to understand the attacks that can be made against it. The major attacks that can be made are phishing, spamming, exploits, malware, etc.

Phishing attacks are designed to steal a person's login and password details so that the cyber criminal can assume control of the victim's social network, email and online bank accounts. Seventy per cent of internet users choose the same password for almost every web service they use. This is why phishing is so effective, as the criminal, by using the same login details, can access multiple private accounts and manipulate them for their own good.

Spamming is when a cyber criminal sends emails designed to make a victim spend money on counterfeit or fake goods. The majority of spam messages are sent, often advertising such as pharmaceutical products or security software, which people believe they need to solve a security issues which doesn't actually exist. Most widely recognized form is email spam. The other spams include IM spam, blog spam, discussion forum spam, cell phone messaging spam, etc.

An exploit is a piece of software, a chunk of data, or sequence of commands that take advantage of a bug, glitch or vulnerability in order to cause unintended or unanticipated behavior to occur on computer software, hardware, or something electronic (usually computerized). This frequently includes things such as gaining control of a computer system or allowing privilege escalation or a denial of service attack.

Malware has become one of the major cyber threats with the expansion of internet. Malware is a relatively new term that gets its name from malicious software. Malware is defined as software designed to infiltrate or damage a computer system without the owner's informed consent. Any software performing malicious actions, including information stealing, spying, etc. can be referred to as malware. Malware is actually a generic definition for all kind of computer threats. Therefore malware refers to malicious software to infect individual computers or an entire organization's network. It exploits target system vulnerabilities, such as a bug in authentic software (e.g., a browser or web application plug-in) that can be hijacked. It can also infect a computer and turn it into a botnet, which means the cyber criminal can control the computer and use it to send malware to others.

As per the definition given by Kaspersky Labs (2017) malware is a type of computer program designed to infect a legitimate user's computer and inflict harm on it in multiple ways [1]. With the expansion of internet diversity of malware is also increasing. Millions of hosts are being attacked because the need of protection is not fulfilled by the anti-virus scanners. According to the Kaspersky Labs (2016) [2], 6,563,145 different hosts were attacked, and 4,000,000 unique malware objects were detected in 2015. The cost of data breaches is predicted by Juniper Research (2016) to increase to $2.1 trillion globally by 2019 [3]. The tools used for attacking are available extensively on the internet now-a-days.

Figure 1 show how the malware is rapidly increasing in volume day-by-day. The x-axis in Figure 1 indicates the year and the y-axis indicates the number of malware specimen generated in the specified year.

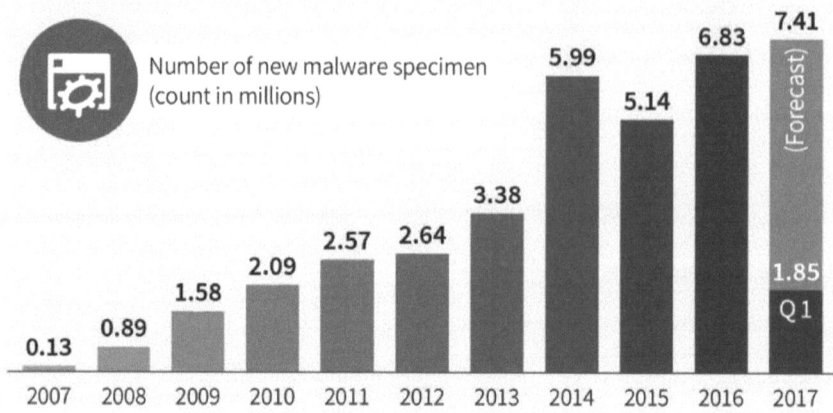

Figure 1. No. of Malware Specification

(Courtesy: -https://www.gdatasoftware.com/blog/2017/04/29666-malware-trends-2017)

Therefore, malware protection of computer systems is one of the most important cyber security tasks for single users and businesses, since even a single attack can result in compromised data and sufficient losses. Massive losses and frequent attacks dictate the need for accurate and timely detection methods. Current static and dynamic methods do not provide efficient detection, especially when dealing with zero-day attacks. For this reason, machine learning-based techniques can be used.

1.1 Types of Malware

This section categorizes malware into different classes depending on its purpose. A simple classification of malware consists of file infectors and stand-alone malware. Another way of classifying malware is based on their particular action: viruses, worms, backdoors, trojans, rootkits, spyware, adware etc. Computer virus detection has evolved into malicious program detection since Cohen first formalized the term computer virus in 1983 [4].

1.1.1 Virus

This is the simplest form of malicious software. It is simply any piece of software that is loaded and launched without user's permission while reproducing itself or infecting (modifying) other software [5]. In other words, Computer virus is a self replicating code (including possibly evolved copies of it) that infects other executable programs. Viruses usually need human intervention for replication and execution.

1.1.1.1 Virus Classification by Target

This section define target as the means exploited by the virus for execution. Based upon the target viruses can be classified into three major classes.

a) Boot Sector Virus

Master Boot Record (Boot sector in DOS) is a piece of code that runs every time a computer system is booted. Boot sector viruses infect the MBR on the disk, hence getting the privilege of getting executed every time the computer system starts up.

b) File Virus

File virus is the most common form of viruses. They infect the file system on a computer. File viruses infect executable programs and are executed every time the infected program is run.

c) Macro Virus

Macro viruses infect documents and templates instead of executable programs. It is written in a macro programming language that is built into applications like Microsoft Word or Excel. Macro virus can be automatically executed every time the document is opened with the application.

1.1.1.2 Virus Classification by Self-Protection Strategy

Self-protection strategy can be defined as the technique used by a virus to avoid detection. In other words, it is known as the anti-antivirus techniques. Based upon self-protection strategies, viruses can be classified into the following categories.

a) No Concealment

Based upon the self-protection strategy the first category can be defined as the one without any concealment. The virus code is clean without any garbage instructions or encryption.

b) Code Obfuscation

Code obfuscation is a technique developed to avoid specific-signature detection. These include adding no-op instructions, unnecessary jumps etc, so the virus code look muddled and the signature fails.

c) Encryption

The next line of defense by the virus writers to defeat signature detection was code encryption. Encrypted viruses use an encrypted virus body and an unencrypted decryption engine. For each infection, the virus is encrypted with a different key to avoid giving a constant signature.

d) Polymorphism

Encrypted viruses are caught by the presence of the unencrypted decryption engine that remains constant for every infection. This is cured by the mutating techniques. Polymorphic viruses feature a mutation engine that generates the decryption engine on the fly. It consists of a decryption engine, a mutation engine and payload. The encrypted virus body and the mutating decryption engine refuse to provide a constant signature.

e) Metamorphism

Metamorphic virus is a self mutating virus in its truest form of the word as it has no constant parts. The virus body itself changes during the infection process and hence the infected file represents a new generation that does not resemble the parent.

f) Stealth

Stealth techniques, also called code armoring, refers to the set of techniques developed by the virus writers to avoid the recent detection methods of activity monitoring, code emulation, etc. The techniques include anti-disassembly, anti-debugging, anti-emulation, anti-heuristics, etc.

1.1.2 Worm

Computer worm is a self replicating stand alone program that spreads on computer networks. Worms usually do not need any extra help from a user to replicate and execute. Worm can spread over the network and replicate to other machines also [6]. The life cycle of worms has been defined by Dan Ellis [7]. Based upon the operations involved in each phase in the life cycle, worms can be classified into different categories. The following taxonomy is used by means of similar factors [8].

1.1.2.1 Activation

Activation defines the means by which a worm is activated onto the target system. This is the first phase in a worm's life cycle. Based upon activation techniques worms can be classified into the following classes.

a) Human Activation

This is the slowest form of activation that requires a human to execute the worm.

b) Human Activity-Based Activation

In this form of activation, the worm execution is based upon some action that the user perform not directly related to the worm such as launching an application program, etc.

c) Scheduled Process Activation

This type of activation depends upon scheduled system processes such as automatic download of software updates, etc.

d) Self Activation

This is the fastest form of activation where a worm initializes its execution by exploiting the vulnerabilities in the programs that are always running such as database or web servers.

1.1.2.2 Payload

The next phase in the worm's life cycle is payload delivery. Payload describes what a worm does after the infection.

a) None

Majority of worms do not carry any payload. The still cause havoc by increasing machine and network traffic load.

b) Internet Remote Control

Some worms open a backdoor on the victim's machine thus allowing others to connect to that machine via internet.

c) Spam-Relays

Some worms convert the victim machine into a spam relay, thus allowing spammers to use it as a server.

1.1.2.3 Target Discovery

In this phase, once the payload is delivered, the worm start looking for new targets to attack.

a) Scanning Worms

Scanning worms scan for targets by scanning sequentially through a block of addresses or by scanning randomly.

b) Flash Worms

Flash worms use a pre-generated target list or a hit list to accelerate the target discovery process.

c) Metaserver Worms

This type of worms uses a list of addresses to infect which is maintained by an external metaserver.

d) Topological Worms

Topological worms try to find the local communication topology by searching through a list of hosts maintained by application programs.

e) Passive Worms

Passive worms rely on user intervention or targets to contact worm for their execution.

1.1.2.4 Propagation

Propagation defines the means by which a worm spreads on a network. Based upon the propagation mechanism worms can be divided into the following categories.

a) Self-Carried

Self carried worms are usually activated by themselves. They copy themselves to the target as part of the infection process.

b) Second Channel

Second channel worm copy their body after the infection by creating a connection from target to host to download the body.

c) Embedded

Embedded worms embed themselves in the normal communication process as a stealth technique.

1.1.3 Trojans

While the words trojan, worm and virus are often used interchangeably, they are not the same. Viruses, worms and trojan horses are all malicious programs that can cause damage to your computer, but there are differences among the three. A trojan horse, also known as a trojan, is a piece of malware, which appears to perform a certain action but in fact performs another such as transmitting a computer virus. At first glance it will appear to be useful software but will actually do damage once installed or run on your computer. Those on the receiving end of a Trojan horse are usually tricked into opening them because they appear to be receiving legitimate software or files from a legitimate source. When a Trojan is activated on your computer, the results can vary. Some Trojans are designed to be more annoying than malicious (like changing your desktop, adding silly active desktop icons) or they can cause serious damage by deleting files and destroying information on your system. Trojans are also known to create a backdoor on your computer that gives malicious users access to your system, possibly allowing confidential or personal information to be compromised. Unlike viruses and worms, Trojans do not reproduce by infecting other files nor do they self-replicate. Simply put, a Trojan horse is not a computer virus. Unlike such malware, it does not propagate by self-replication but relies heavily on the exploitation of an end-user. It is instead a categorical attribute, which can encompass many different forms of codes. Therefore, a computer worm or virus may be a Trojan horse. The term is derived from the classical story of the Trojan horse.

Therefore Trojan horses or simply trojans are programs that perform some malicious activity under the guise of some normal program. This malware class is used to define the malware types that aim to appear as legitimate software. Because of this, the general spreading vector utilized in this class is social engineering, i.e. making people think that they are downloading the legitimate software [9].

1.1.3.1 How Trojans work

Trojans usually consist of two parts, a Client and a Server. The server is run on the victim's machine and listens for connections from a Client, which is used by the attacker. When the server is run on a machine it will listen on a specific port or multiple ports for connections from a Client. In order for an attacker to connect to the server they must have the IP Address of the computer where the server is being run. Some Trojans have the IP Address of the computer they are running on sent to the attacker via email or another form or communication. Once a connection is made to the server, the client can then send commands to the server; the server will then execute these commands on the victim's machine. Today, with NAT (Network Address Translation) infrastructure being very common, most computers cannot be reached by their external IP address. Therefore many Trojans now connect to the computer of the attacker, which has been set up to take the connections, instead of the attacker connecting to his or her victim. This is called a 'reverse-connect' Trojan. Many Trojans nowadays also bypass many personal firewall installed on the victims computer (e.g. Poison Ivy).

Trojans are extremely simple to create in many programming languages. A simple Trojan in Visual Basic or C# using Visual Studio can be achieved in 10 lines of code or under. Probably the most famous Trojan horse is the AIDS TROJAN DISK that was sent to about 7000 research organizations on a diskette. When the Trojan was introduced on the system, it scrambled the name of all files (except a few) and filled the empty areas of the disk completely. The program offered a recovery solution in exchange of a bounty. Thus, malicious cryptography was born.

1.1.3.2 Trojans types

Trojans are generally the programs that pose as legitimate programs on your computer and add a subversive functionality to it. That's when it's said a program is Trojaned. Common functions of Trojans include, but are not limited to, the following:

a) Remote Access Trojans

These are probably the most widely used trojans, just because they give the attackers the power to do more things on the victim's machine than the victim itself while being in front of the machine. Most of these trojans are often a combination of the other variations described below. The idea of these trojans is to give the attacker a total access to someone's machine and therefore access to files, private conversations, accounting data, etc.

b) Password Sending Trojans

The purpose of these trojans is to copy all the cached passwords and also look for other passwords you're entering and then send them to a specific mail address without the user noticing anything. Passwords for ICQ, IRC, FTP, HTTP or any other application that require a user to enter a login password are being sent back to the attacker's email address, which in most cases is located at some free web based email provider.

c) Keyloggers

These trojans are very simple. The only thing they do is logging the keystrokes of the victim and then letting the attacker search for passwords or other sensitive data in the log file. Most of them come with two functions like online and offline recording. Of course, they could be configured to send the log file to a specific email address on a schedule basis.

d) Destructive

The only function of these trojans is to destroy and delete files. This makes them very simple and easy to use. They can automatically delete all the system files on your machine. The trojan is being activated by the attacker or sometimes works like a logic bomb and starts on a specific day and at specific hour. Denial of Service (DoS) Attack Trojan is getting very popular these days, giving the attacker the power to start DoS when having enough victims, of course. The main idea is that if you have 200 ADSL users infected and start attacking the victim simultaneously, this will generate a lot of traffic (more than the victim's bandwidth, in most cases) and its access to the internet will be shut down.

e) Mail-Bomb Trojan

This is another variation of a DoS trojan whose main aim is to infect as many machines as possible and simultaneously attack specific email address/addresses with random subjects and contents which cannot be filtered.

f) Proxy/Wingate Trojans

The interesting feature implemented in many trojans is turning the victim's computer into a proxy/wingate server available to the whole world or to the attacker only. It's used for anonymous Telnet, ICQ, IRC, etc., and also for registering domains with stolen credit cards and for many other illegal activities. This gives the attacker complete anonymity and the chance to do everything from your computer, and if he/she gets caught, the trace leads back to you.

g) FTP Trojans

These trojans are probably the most simple ones and are kind of outdated as the only thing they do is to open port 21 (the port for FTP transfers) and let everyone or just the attacker connect to your machine. Newer versions are password protected, so only the one who infected you may connect to your computer.

h) Software Detection Killers

There are such functionalities built into some trojans, but there are also separate programs that will kill ZoneAlarm, Norton Anti-Virus and many other (popular anti-virus/firewall) programs that protect your machine. When they are disabled, the attacker will have full access to your machine to perform some illegal activity, use your computer to attack others and often disappear. Even though you may notice that these programs are not working or functioning properly, it will take you some time to remove the trojan, install the new software, configure it and get back online with some sense of security.

1.1.4 Adware

The only purpose of this malware type is displaying advertisements on the computer. Often adware can be seen as a subclass of spyware and it will very unlikely lead to dramatic results. Adware is the name given to programs that are designed to display advertisements on your computer, redirect your search requests to advertising websites and collect marketing-type data about you – for example, the types of websites that you visit – so that customized adverts can be displayed. Adware collects data with your consent, should not be confused with Trojan spyware programs that collect information, without your permission. If Adware does not notify you that it is gathering information, it is regarded as malicious – for example, malware that uses Trojan-Spy behavior.

1.1.5 Spyware

Spyware is computer software that is installed surreptitiously on a personal computer to intercept or take partial control over the user's interaction with the computer, without the user's informed consent. Actions of spyware include tracking search history to send personalized advertisements, tracking activities to sell them to the third parties subsequently [10].

1.1.6 Rootkit

Its functionality enables the attacker to access the data with higher permissions than is allowed. For example, it can be used to give an unauthorized user administrative access. Rootkits always hide its existence and quite often are unnoticeable on the system, making the detection and therefore removal incredibly hard [11].

1.1.7 Backdoor

The backdoor is a type of malware that provides an additional secret "entrance" to the system for attackers. By itself, it does not cause any harm but provides attackers with broader attack surface. Because of this, backdoors are never used independently. Usually, they are preceding malware attacks of other types.

1.1.8 Keylogger

The idea behind this malware class is to log all the keys pressed by the user, and, therefore, store all data, including passwords, bank card numbers and other sensitive information [12].

1.1.9 Ransomware

This type of malware aims to encrypt all the data on the machine and ask a victim to transfer some money to get the decryption key. Usually, a machine infected by ransomware is "frozen" as the user cannot open any file, and the desktop picture is used to provide information on attacker's demands [13].

1.1.10 Remote Administration Tools

This malware type allows an attacker to gain access to the system and make possible modifications as if it was accessed physically. Intuitively, it can be described as in the example of the TeamViewer, but with malicious intentions.

1.1.11 Botnet

A program similar to backdoor, but with a difference that the information systems affected build a network of bots that receive commands from a server known as command-and-control. A bot infestation doesn't actively harm your computer, but it makes your system complicit in harming others. It quietly hides itself until the owner, or "bot herder", broadcasts a command. Then, along with hundreds or thousands of others, it does whatever it's told. Bots are often used to send spam, so the spammer's own systems aren't implicated.

1.1.12 Scareware

Not all antivirus programs are what they seem. Some are actually fakes, rogue programs that don't protect your security and do harm your bank balance. At best these programs offer no real protection; at worst they include actively harmful elements. They work hard to scare you into paying for registration, so they're often called scareware. If you do register, you've both wasted your money and handed your credit card information to crooks. Avoiding scareware gets more and more difficult as the programs get more refined.

These categories aren't mutually exclusive. For example, a single threat might virus-style, steal your personal information like spyware, and use rootkit technology to hide itself from your antivirus. A scareware program is a kind of Trojan, and it might also steal private data.

The term malware encompasses all of these types of malicious software. Any program whose purpose is harmful is a malware program, pure and simple. Industry groups like the Anti-Malware Testing Standards Organization (AMTSO) use this term for clarity, but the general public still asks for antivirus, not anti-malware. The antivirus should protect against any and all malware.

1.2 Malware Classification Tree

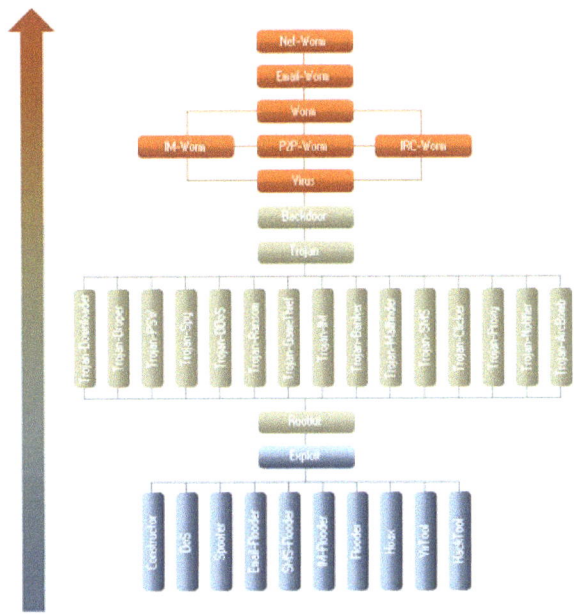

Figure 2. Malware Classification tree

(Courtesy: -https://usa.kaspersky.com/resource-center/threats/malware-classifications)

Kaspersky's classification system gives each detected object a clear description and a specific location in the 'classification tree' shown in figure 2. In the 'classification tree' diagram:

- The types of behavior that pose the least threat are shown in the lower area of the diagram.
- The types of behavior that pose a greater threat are displayed in the upper part of the diagram.
- The 'classification tree' shows that each behavior has been assigned its own threat level.

- In the 'classification tree' the behaviors that pose a higher risk outrank those behaviors that represent a lower risk.

1.3 Classification Methods

This section briefly describes the various classification methods used in order to categorize the malwares. The supervised methods used are Naïve Bayes classifier, J48 Decision Trees and Support Vector Machines, whereas the unsupervised method is an adaptation of the K-means clustering method.

1.3.1 Supervised Methods

1.3.1.1 Naïve Bayes Classifier

The Naïve Bayes classifier works on a simple, but comparatively intuitive concept. Also, in some cases it is also seen that Naïve Bayes outperforms many other comparatively complex algorithms. It makes use of the variables contained in the data sample, by observing them individually, independent of each other.

The Naïve Bayes classifier is based on the Bayes rule of conditional probability. It makes use of all the attributes contained in the data, and analyses them individually as though they are equally important and independent of each other. For example, consider that the training data consists of various animals (say elephants, monkeys and giraffes), and the classifier has to classify any new instance that it encounters. It is known that elephants have attributes like they have a trunk, huge tusks, a short tail, are extremely big, etc. Monkeys are short in size, jump around a lot, and can climb trees; whereas giraffes are tall, have a long neck and short ears.

The Naïve Bayes classifier will consider each of these attributes separately when classifying a new instance. So, when checking to see if the new instance is an elephant, the Naïve Bayes classifier will not check whether it has a trunk and has huge tusks and is large. Rather, it will separately check whether the new instance has a trunk, whether it has tusks, whether it is large, etc. It works under the assumption that one attribute works independently of the other attributes contained by the sample.

1.3.1.2 J48 Decision Trees

A decision tree is a predictive machine-learning model that decides the target value (dependent variable) of a new sample based on various attribute values of the available data. The internal nodes of a decision tree denote the different attributes; the branches between the nodes tell us the possible values that these attributes can have in the observed samples, while the terminal nodes tell us the final value (classification) of the dependent variable.

The attribute that is to be predicted is known as the dependent variable, since its value depends upon, or is decided by, the values of all the other attributes. The other attributes, which help in predicting the value of the dependent variable, are known as the independent variables in the dataset.

The J48 Decision tree classifier follows the following simple algorithm. In order to classify a new item, it first needs to create a decision tree based on the attribute values of the available training data. So, whenever it encounters a set of items (training set) it identifies the attribute that discriminates the various instances most clearly. This feature which is able to tell most about the data instances so that they can be best classified is said to have the highest information gain. Now, among the possible values of this feature, if there is any value for which there is no ambiguity, that is, for which the data instances falling within its category have the same value for the target variable, then we terminate that branch and assign to it the target value that we have obtained.

For the other cases, we then look for another attribute that gives us the highest information gain. Hence we continue in this manner until we either get a clear decision of what combination of attributes gives us a particular target value, or we run out of attributes. In the event that we run out of attributes, or if we cannot get an unambiguous result from the available information, we assign this branch a target value that the majority of the items under this branch possess.

Now that we have the decision tree, we follow the order of attribute selection as we have obtained for the tree. By checking all the respective attributes and their values with those seen in the decision tree model, we can assign or predict the target value of this new instance.

1.3.1.3 Support Vector Machines

Support Vector Machines are supervised learning methods used for classification, as well as regression. The advantage of Support Vector Machines is that they can make use of certain kernels in order to transform the problem, such that we can apply linear classification techniques to non-linear data. Applying the kernel equations arranges the data instances in such a way within the multi-dimensional space, that there is a hyper-plane that separates data instances of one kind from those of another.

The kernel equations may be any function that transforms the linearly non-separable data in one domain into another domain where the instances become linearly separable. Kernel equations may be linear, quadratic, Gaussian, or anything else that achieves this particular purpose.

The data is divided into two distinct categories; the aim is to get the best hyper-plane to separate the two types of instances. This hyper-plane is important because it decides the target variable value for future predictions. A hyper-plane should be decided that maximizes the margin between the support vectors on either side of the plane. Support vectors are those instances that are either on the separating planes on each side, or a little on the wrong side.

One important thing to note about Support Vector Machines is that the data to be separated needs to be binary. Even if the data is not binary, Support Vector Machines handles it as though it is, and completes the analysis through a series of binary assessments on the data.

The data instances which were not linearly separable in the original domain become linearly separable in the new domain, due to the application of a function (kernel) that transforms the position of the data points from one domain to another. This is the basic idea behind Support Vector Machines and their kernel techniques. Whenever a new instance is encountered in the original domain, the same kernel function is applied to this instance too, and its position in the new domain is found out. This position determines the binary target value to which the new instance belongs.

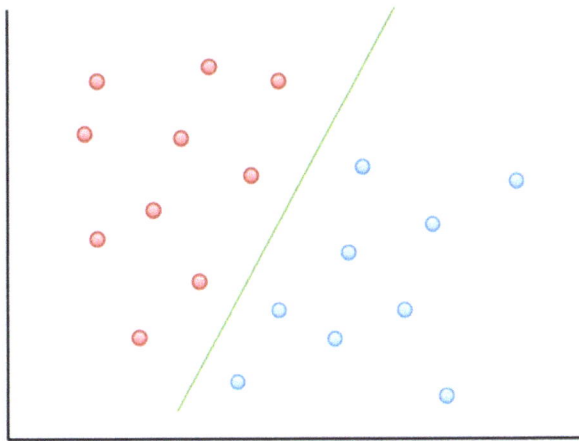

Figure 3. SVM scheme

(Courtesy: -https: //eight2late.wordpress.com/2017/02/07/a-gentle-introduction-to-support-vector-machines-using-r)

In many cases, it is often seen that Support Vector Machines perform the best among all machine-learning methods.

1.3.1.4 K-nearest neighbors

K-Nearest Neighbors (KNN) is one of the simplest, though, accurate machine learning algorithms. KNN is a non-parametric algorithm, meaning that it does not make any assumptions about the data structure. In real world problems, data rarely obeys the general theoretical assumptions, making non-parametric algorithms a good solution for such problems. KNN model representation is as simple as the dataset – there is no learning required the entire training set is stored.

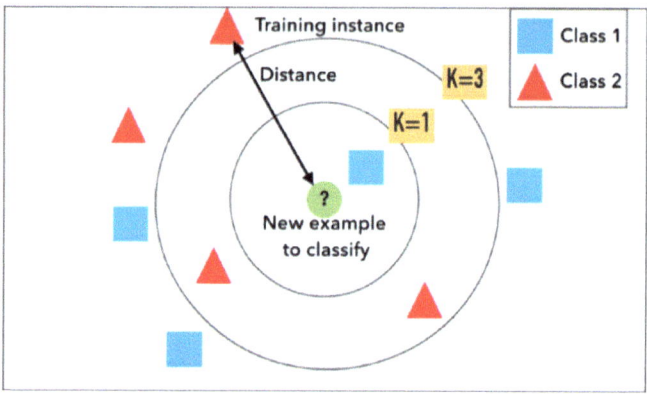

Figure 4. KNN Scheme

(Courtesy:-https://sflscientific.com/data-science-blog/2016/6/4/time-series-analysis-fitbit-using-dtw-and-knn)

KNN can be used for both classification and regression problems. In both problems, the prediction is based on the k training instances that are closest to the input instance. In the KNN classification problem, the output would be a class, to which the input instance belongs, predicted by the majority vote of the k closest neighbors. In the regression problem, the output would be the property value, which is generally a mean value of the k nearest neighbors. The schematic example is outlined in Figure 4.

Different distance measurement methods are used for finding the closest neighbors. The popular ones include Hamming Distance, Manhattan Distance, and Minkowski distance.

For the classification problems, the output can also be presented as a set of probabilities of an instance belonging to the class. For example, for binary problems, the probabilities can be calculated like $P(0)=N0/N0+N1$, where $P(0)$ is the probability of the 0 class membership and $N0$, $N1$ are numbers of neighbors belonging to the classes 0 and 1 respectively [14].

The value of k plays a crucial role in the accuracy prediction of the algorithm. However, selecting the k value is a non-trivial task. Smaller values of k will most likely result in lower accuracy, especially in the datasets with much noise, since every instance of the training set now has a higher weight during the decision process. Larger values of k lower the performance of the algorithm. In addition to that, if the value is too high, the model will be overfit, making the class boundaries less distinct and resulting in lower accuracy again. As a general approach, it is advised to select k using the formula below:

$$k=\sqrt{n}$$

For classification problems with an even number of classes, it is advised to choose an odd k since this will eliminate the possibility of a tie during the majority vote.

The drawback of the KNN algorithm is the bad performance on the unevenly distributed datasets. Thus, if one class vastly dominates the other ones, it is more likely to have more neighbors of that class due to their large number, and, therefore, make incorrect predictions [15].

1.3.1.5 N-grams

N-grams is the most common feature used by the data mining methods. They are basically a set of co-occurring words within a given window and when computing the n-grams you typically move one word forward (although you can move X words forward in more advanced scenarios).

For example, for the sentence *"The cow jumps over the moon"*. If N=2 (known as bigrams), then the ngrams would be:

- the cow
- cow jumps
- jumps over
- over the
- the moon

So you have 5 n-grams in this case. Notice that we moved from the->cow to cow->jumps to jumps->over, etc, essentially moving one word forward to generate the next bigram.

If N=3, the n-grams would be:

- the cow jumps
- cow jumps over
- jumps over the
- over the moon

So you have 4 n-grams in this case. When N=1, this is referred to as unigrams and this is essentially the individual words in a sentence. When N=2, this is called bigrams and when N=3 this is called trigrams. When N>3 this is usually referred to as four grams or five grams and so on. If X=no. of words in a given sentence K, the number of n-grams for sentence K would be:

$$Ngrams_K = X - (N-1)$$

Use of n-grams is for developing features for supervised Machine Learning models such as SVMs, MaxEnt models, Naive Bayes, etc. The idea is to use tokens such as bigrams in the feature space instead of just unigrams. Here, n-grams is described as a general term for both overlapping and non-overlapping byte sequences.

1.3.2 Unsupervised Methods

1.3.2.1 K-means clustering algorithm

Clustering is the process in which we divide the available data instances into a given number of sub-groups. These sub-groups are called clusters, and hence the name "Clustering". To put it simply, the K-means algorithm outlines a method to cluster a particular set of instances into K different clusters, where K is a positive integer. It should be noted here that the K-means clustering algorithm requires knowing the number of clusters from the user. It cannot identify the number of clusters by itself. K-means is one of the simplest unsupervised learning algorithms that solve the well known clustering problem. The procedure follows a simple and easy way to classify a given data set through a certain number of clusters (assume k clusters) fixed before.

The K-means clustering algorithm starts by placing K centroids as far away from each other as possible within the available space. Then each of the available data instances is assigned a particular centroid, depending on a metric like Euclidian distance, Manhattan distance, Minkowski distance, etc. The position of the centroid is recalculated every time an instance is added to the cluster and this continues until all the instances are grouped into the final required number of clusters. Since recalculating the cluster centroids may alter the cluster membership, the cluster memberships are also verified once the position of the centroid changes. This process continues till there is no further change in the cluster membership, and there is as little change in the positions of the centroids as possible.

The initial position of the centroids is thus very important since this position affects all the future steps in the K-means clustering algorithm. Hence, it is always advisable to keep the cluster centers as far away from each other as possible. If there are too many clusters, then clusters that closely resemble each other and are in the vicinity of each other are clubbed together. If there are too few clusters then clusters that are too big and may contain two or more sub-groups of different data instances are divided. The K-means clustering algorithm is thus a simple to understand, fairly intuitive method by which we can divide the available data into sub-categories. SenseClusters is a variation of K-means clustering algorithm. However, SenseClusters has the facility of automatically identifying the number of clusters that the data may comprise of. To classify the email messages into different user-defined folders SenseClusters can be used. SenseClusters is a freely available package of Perl programs, developed at the University of Minnesota Duluth, which can be used for automatic text and document classification. The advantage of SenseClusters is that it does not need any training data; it makes use of unsupervised learning methods in order to classify the available data.

The accuracy of the unsupervised method is not far behind that of the supervised methods. In fact, in a couple of cases, the unsupervised method outperformed many of the supervised methods. Training set is also not required for unsupervised learning methods.

1.4 Difference between K-nearest neighbor and K-means clustering algorithm

In short, the algorithms are trying to accomplish different goals. K-nearest neighbor is a subset of supervised learning classification (or regression) algorithms (it takes a bunch of labeled points and uses them to learn how to label other points). It is supervised because you are trying to classify a point based on the known classification of other points. In contrast, K-means is a subset of unsupervised learning clustering algorithms (it takes a bunch of unlabeled points and tries to group them into clusters). It is unsupervised because the points have no external classification.

The *k* in each case means different things. In K-NN, the *k* represents the number of neighbors who have a vote in determining a new point's position. The *k* in K-means, determine the number of clusters we want to end up.

In a K-NN algorithm, a test sample is given as the class of majority of its nearest neighbors. For example, if we have three classes and the goal is to find a class label for the unknown example *k* then, by using the Euclidean distance and a value of *k=5* neighbors, the unknown sample is classified to the category of the most voted neighbors.

The situation with K-means is that, given some data you will cluster them in k-groups or clusters. The initial step of the algorithm is to randomly spawn *k* centroids (centers). During each iteration, the center of each cluster is moved slightly to minimize the objective function. The algorithm will terminate if the iterations are maximized or if the centroids stop to move.

1.5 Malware Detection Techniques

1.5.1 Signature Based Detection

Signature based detection is a simple and most commonly used technique in antivirus software. They are popular because of accurate detection, simplicity and their speed. In signature based detection, the scanner scans each executable and looks for specific string or pattern of bits (signatures). Antivirus software has a database of signatures for different viruses. By comparing the signature, it detects the virus. The disadvantage is that only the known malware can be detected. If the signature is not known, malware cannot be detected. The signature file must be kept up to date. By using simple code obfuscation techniques, malware can easily evade the signature based detection.

1.5.2 Anomaly Based Detection

The problem of detecting new malwares in signature based detection can be overcome using anomaly based detection. Heuristic methods are implemented to detect anomalous behavior. This technique comprises of two phases - the training phase and the detection phase. In the training phase, the model is trained with the normal behavior. Anything other than the normal behavior is considered as malicious behavior. However, there can be more false positives in this technique.

1.5.3 Heuristic Analysis or Pro-Active Defense

Heuristic scanning is similar to signature scanning, except that instead of looking for specific signatures, heuristic scanning looks for certain instructions or commands within a program that are not found in typical application programs. As a result, a heuristic engine is able to detect potentially malicious functionality in new, previously unexamined, malicious functionality such as the replication mechanism of a virus, the distribution routine of a worm or the payload of a Trojan.

Few of the common heuristic scanning techniques:

1.5.3.1 Hidden Markov Model Based Detection

Hidden Markov models (HMMs) are generally used for statistical pattern analysis. They can be used in speech recognition, malware detection and biological sequence analysis. In this section an overview of the introduction to HMM and its usage in detection of malware is described.

A statistical model that has states and known probabilities of the state transitions is called a Markov model. In such a Markov model, the states are visible to the observer. In contrast, a hidden Markov model (HMM) has states that are not directly observable. HMM is a machine learning technique. HMM acts as a state machine. Every state is associated with a probability distribution for observing a set of observation symbols. The transitions between the states have fixed probabilities. We can train an HMM using the observation sequences to represent a set of data. We can match an observation sequence against a trained HMM to determine the probability of seeing such a sequence. If the probability is high, the observation sequence is similar to the training sequences. HMMs are used in protein modeling. HMM is also used to detect certain types of software piracy. There is a lot of previous work done on the use of HMM for malware detection. When an HMM is trained, it can be used to distinguish between a malware and a benign file. The dataset is tested against the trained models. There is a range of values of scores for which the scores of the malware and the benign files do not overlap. This is known as threshold. Using this threshold, the malware can be distinguished from the benign files.

1.5.4 Genetic Signature Detection

This technique is particularly designed to locate variations of viruses. Several viruses are recreated and make themselves known by a variety of names, but essentially come from the same family (or classification). Genetic detection uses previous antivirus definitions to locate these similar "cousins" even if they use a slightly different name or include some unusual characters. The best way to illustrate this idea is with identical twins. They may have slightly different fingerprints, but their DNA is identical. Heuristic Detection is an effective way to locate unknown threats for the most up-to-date real time protection, but there are downsides. Obviously this sort of scanning and analysis can take some time, which may slow-down system performance. The main concern with heuristic detection is that it often increases false positives. False positives are when the antivirus software determines a file is malicious (and quarantines or deletes it) when in reality it is perfectly fine and/or desired. Because some files may look like viruses but really aren't, they are restricted and stopped from working on your computer.

1.6 Malware Detection Tools

Cybercriminals are putting forth every effort to make malware difficult to detect. In the ongoing war against malware threats, tools are needed that will baseline your system, detect vulnerabilities, and remove existing malware. Below few malware detection tools are mentioned.

1.6.1 Microsoft Process Explorer (formerly Sysinternals)

Process Explorer provides an excellent way to determine what processes are running on a computer. It also describes the function of each process. Process Explorer can be used to create a baseline of the running processes used by the computer when it's operating correctly. If for some reason the computer starts behaving poorly, run Process Explorer again and compare the scans. Any differences will be good places to start looking for malware.

1.6.2 Trend Micro's HiJackThis

HiJackThis is Process Explorer on steroids. Its use requires the complete familiarity with operating systems. Running HiJackThis before having malware problems creates a great reference baseline, making it easy to spot changes.

Several Web sites offer online applications that will automatically analyze the log file from HiJackThis, pointing out possible conflicts. Examples of websites are HiJackThis.de Security and NetworkTechs.com. If trained experts help is available, WindowSecurity.com's HiJackThis forum can also be used.

1.6.3 Kaspersky's GetSystemInfo

Kaspersky has an application similar to HiJackThis called GetSystemInfo. Kaspersky has an online parser. After uploading the log file, the parser will point out any disparities. GetSystemInfo, like the other scanners, is a good way to keep track of what's on the computer.

1.6.4 Microsoft Baseline Security Analyzer

Anti-malware includes any program that combats malware, whether it's real-time protection or detection and removal of existing malware. Vulnerability scanners proactively detect vulnerabilities so that malware can't gain a foothold. Microsoft Baseline Security Analyzer (MBSA) is a vulnerability scanner that detects insecure configuration settings and checks all installed Microsoft products for missing security updates.

1.6.5 Secunia inspection scanners

Secunia's scanners are similar to MBSA when it comes to Microsoft products. But unlike MBSA, Secunia products also scan hundreds of third-party applications, which give Secunia a distinct advantage. All the Secunia scanners, online and client-side, have an intuitive way of determining what is wrong and how to rectify it. They usually offer a link to the application's Web page, where the update can be downloaded.

1.6.6 Antivirus programs

Antivirus programs can detect malicious code. But still some malcode can be missed by one antivirus program whereas others scanners can find it. Choosing the correct antivirus application depends upon ones choice. Anti-malware is capable of both detecting and removing malware. Scanners use signature files and heuristics to detect malware. Malware developers know all about each and can morph their code, which then nullifies signature files and confuses heuristics. That's why malware scanners aren't the cure-all answer.

1.6.7 Microsoft's Malicious Software Removal Tool

Malicious Software Removal Tool (MSRT) is a good general malware removal tool, simply because Microsoft should know whether the scanned code is theirs or not. Advantages of MSRT are:

- The scan and removal process is automated.
- Windows Update keeps the signature file database current automatically.
- It has the advantage of being an OEM product, thus it's less intrusive and more likely to be accepted by management.

1.6.8 SUPER Antispyware

SUPER Antispyware is another general purpose scanner that does a good job of detecting and removing most malware. SUPER Antispyware is the only scanner capable of completely removing antivirus 2009 (malware).

1.6.9 Malware byte's Anti-Malware

Malware bytes Anti-Malware (MBAM) malware scanner is the most successful scanner. Still, MBAM does not catch everything. It misses some of the more sophisticated malware, especially rootkits.

1.6.10 GMER

It's hard to find rootkit malware. Fortunately, GMER is one of the best when it comes to detecting and removing rootkits.

CHAPTER 2
LITERATURE SURVEY

A lot of previous work is done on detection and classification of malware. This chapter discusses some attempts made for malware classification, which include usage of structured control workflow and some data mining methods

2.1 Data Mining

Data mining has been the focus of many virus researchers in the recent years to detect unknown viruses. A number of classifiers have been built and shown to have very high accuracy rates. The most common method of applying data mining techniques for malware detection start from generating a feature set. These features include hexadecimal byte sequences (later termed as n-grams), instruction sequences, API/system call sequences etc. The number of features extracted from the files is usually very high. Several techniques from text classification [16] have been employed to select the best features. Some other features include printable strings extracted from the files and some operating system dependent features such as DLL information. The following sections provide literature review of data mining techniques used in the virus detection research. Some of these methods might use activity monitoring as a data collection method but data mining remains the principal detection method.

2.1.1 Dynamic Misuse Detection

The first major work that used data mining techniques for malware research was an automation of signature extraction for viruses by [17]. The viruses were executed in a secured environment to infect decoy programs. Candidate signatures of variable length were extracted by analyzing the infected regions in these programs that remained invariant from one program to another. Signatures with lowest estimated false positive probabilities were chosen as the best signatures.

To handle large, rare sequences, a trigram approach was borrowed from speech recognition where the large sequence was broken down into trigrams. Then, a simple approximation formula was used to estimate the probability of a long sequence by combining the measured frequencies of the shorter sequences from which it is composed. To measure algorithms effectiveness candidate signatures were generated and their estimated and actual probabilities were compared. Most of the signatures fell short of this criterion and were considered bad signatures. Another measure of effectiveness was false positive record of signatures, which was reported to be minimal. However no numerical values were provided for estimated and actual probability comparison and false positives.

2.1.2 Dynamic Hybrid Detection

The pioneering work of Tesauro et al. [18] extended the n-grams analysis to detect boot sector viruses using neural networks. The n-grams were selected based upon the frequencies of occurrence in viral and benign programs. Feature reduction was obtained by generating a 4-cover such that each virus in the dataset should have at least 4 of these frequent n-grams present in order for the n-grams to be included in the dataset. A validation set classification accuracy of 80-85% was obtained on viral boot sector while clean boot sectors received a 100% classification.

In the continuation of their work they [18], [19] used n-grams as features to build multiple neural network classifiers and adopted a voting strategy to predict the final outcome. Their dataset consisted of 53902 clean files and 72 variant sets of different viruses. For clean files, n-grams were extracted from the entire file while only those portions of a virus file are considered that remain constant through different variants of the same virus. A simple threshold pruning algorithm was used to reduce the number of n-grams to use as features. The results they reported are not very promising but it still presents a thorough work using neural networks.

2.1.3 Static Anomaly Detection

Wang et al. [20] proposed a method of classifying various file types based upon their fileprints. An n-gram analysis method was used and the distribution of n-grams in a file was used as its fileprint. The distribution was given by byte value frequency distribution and standard deviation. These fileprints represented the normal profile of the files and were compared against fileprints taken at a later time using simplified Mahalanobis distance. A large distance indicated a different n-gram distribution and hence maliciousness.

2.1.4 Static Hybrid Detection

The most recent work that brought the data mining techniques for malware detection to the limelight was done by [21]. They used three different types of features and a variety of classifiers to detect malicious programs. Their primary dataset contained 3265 malicious and 1001 clean programs. They applied RIPPER (a rule based system) to the DLL dataset. Strings data was used to fit a Naive Bayes classifier while n-grams were used to train a Multi-Naive Bayes classifier with a voting strategy. No n-gram reduction algorithm was reported to be used. Instead data set partitioning was used and 6 Naive-Bayes classifiers were trained on each partition of the data. They used different features to built different classifiers that do not pose a fair comparison among the classifiers. Naive-Bayes using strings gave the best accuracy in their model.

Extending the same ideas [22], Malicious Email Filter (MEF) was created, that integrated the scheme described in [21] into a Unix email server. A large dataset consisting of 3301 malicious and 1000 benign programs was used to train and test a Naive-Bayes classifier. N-grams were extracted by parsing the hexdump output. For feature reduction the dataset was partitioned into 16 subsets. Each subset is independently trained on a different classifier and a voting strategy was used to obtain the final outcome. The classifier achieved 97.7% detection rate on novel malwares and 99.8% on known ones. Together with [21], this paved the way for a plethora of research in malware detection using data mining approaches.

A similar approach was used by [23], where they built different classifiers including Instancebased Learner, TFIDF, Naive-Bayes, Support vector machines, Decision tree, boosted Naive-Bayes, SVMs and boosted decision tree. Their primary dataset consisted of 1971 clean and 1651 malicious programs. Information gain was used to choose top 500 n-grams as features. Best efficiency was reported using the boosted decision tree J48 algorithm.

Abou-Assaleh et al. [24] created class profiles of various lengths using different n-gram sizes. The class profile length was defined by the number of most frequent n-grams within the class. These frequent n-grams from both classes were combined to form, what they termed as relevant n-grams, for each profile length. Experiments were conducted on a set of 250 benign and 250 malicious programs. For classification, Dampster-Shafer theory of Evidence was used to combine SVM, decision tree and IBK classifiers. They compared their work with [23] and reported better results. In a related work, [25] used a Common N-Gram classification method to create malware profile signatures. Similar class profiles of various lengths using different n-gram sizes were created. The class profile length was defined by the number of most frequent n-grams with their normalized frequencies. A k-nearest neighbor algorithm was used to match a new profile instance with a set of already created signature profiles. They experimented with combinations of different profile lengths and different n-gram sizes. A five-fold cross validation method gave 91% classification accuracy.

Building upon their previous work in [26], Yoo et al. [27] experimented with a larger data collection with 790 infected and 80 benign files, thus landing in static hybrid detection category. N-grams were extracted from octal dump of the program, instead of usual hexdump and then converted to short integer values for SOM input. Using the SOM algorithms, Virus Detector was created that was used as a detection tool, instead of a visualization tool. Virus Detector achieved 84% detection with a 30% false positive rate. The technique is able to cater polymorphic and encrypted viruses.

In a recent n-grams based static hybrid detection approach [28] used intra-family and interfamily support to select and reduce the number of features. First, the most frequent n-grams within each virus family were selected. Then the list was pruned to contain only those features that have a support threshold higher than a given value amongst these families. This was done for various n-gram sizes. Experiments were carried out on a set of 3000 programs, 1552 of which were viruses, belonging to 110 families, and 1448 were benign programs. With ID3, J4 decision tree, Naive Bayes and SMO classifiers, they compared their results with [21] and claimed better overall efficiency. In search of optimal feature selection criteria, they experimented with different n-gram sizes and various values of intra-family and inter-family selection thresholds. They reported better results with shorter sequences. For longer sequences, a low inter-family threshold gave better performance. Better performance was also noted, when features were in excess of 200.

2.1.5 Static Misuse Detection

Yoo el al. [26] presented a static misuse method to detect viruses using self organizing maps (SOM). They claimed that each virus has its own DNA like character that changes the SOM projection of the program that it infects. N-grams were extracted from the infected programs and SOMs were trained on this data. Since the method only looks for change in the SOM projection as a result of virus infection, it is able to detect polymorphic and metamorphic malwares, even in the encrypted state. Experiments were performed on a small set of 14 viral samples. The algorithm was successfully able to detect virus patterns in the infected files.

2.2 Machine Learning

Various machine learning algorithms (Perceptron, MeanShift, DBSCAN, etc) have been conducted and developed regarding the detection, identification and classification of unidentified and unrecognized malware into known malware families. Schultz et al. [29] applied and extracted three signature-based characteristics for malware classification: Byte sequences Portable Executables (PE) and computer variables most likely strings. The directory of DLLs, function calls and several system calls employed within each DLL used by the file and executable, are reversed engineered and abstracted from DLL records and data that are enclosed to Portable Executable files. Computer variables are processed and analyzed from the executable files established by the text computer variables that are encrypted in program files. All the sequences of n bytes that were being modified and derived from an executable file are named in general as byte sequence.

Their performance results were improved by Kolter and Maloof [30] using data mining methodologies and n-gram as a feature to detect malware. The algorithms chosen were Naïve Bayes, Support Vector Machines, Decision Trees with the last giving the best classification results.

Need for automation on malware classification was stressed by Kong and Yan in 2013 [31]. Authors proposed a framework that depends on function call graph of malware. After finding a good way to extract the features based on function call graph for each malware sample, they used distance metrics to find the similarities between two malware programs. These metrics clustered and categorized the malware samples to same malware and class family while using a limited range kept the different groups separated. Having tested that approach an aggregation of classifying algorithms was utilized and suggested that learns from pair wise malware distances to categorize malware into certain malware families.

Tian, Islam, Batten, & Versteeg in [32] focused on classifying Trojans that use function length frequency. The amount of bytes that determines the function length is in the cipher. The performance of the algorithms shows that the function range along with its frequency are meaningful in the field of identification of malware families and is associated with other characteristics for malware classification regarding performance. WEKA library provides such algorithm for categorizing malware.

A different approach that was suggested from Santos in [33] mentions that a reasonable number of supervised executable files for malicious and benign samples were used in a semi-supervised methodology for identification and discovery of zero day exploits. This methodology utilizes and tries to perform machine learning using a lot of supervised and unsupervised cases and experiments. Learning with Local and Global Consistency (LLGC) which is a semi-supervised model, is employed, which can be trained from supervised and unsupervised data and provides an answer regarding the basic architecture presented by both supervised and unsupervised situations. An n-gram method characterizes and defines executables. Moreover, researchers conduct and assess the ideal amount of supervised situations and the effect of these situations regarding accuracy. Goal achieved of this inquiry and investigation is to decrease the amount of necessary supervised cases while achieving significant accuracy. The only downgrade is that supervised training methodologies were shown and presented better performance above or near 90%.

Another interesting research was done by Siddiqui, Wang, & Lee in [34]. Their intention was to detect worms while examining the packets from traffic and find samples that are not yet analyzed and submitted to vendors, (also known as a term in the wild, another exciting field of detection). Before reverse engineering the samples, compilers and packers are identified and discovered. Decision Tree and Random Forest are utilized for classification and to make sequence reduction.

Zolkipli & Jantan in [35] wanted to see malware classification from the point of view of malware behavior analysis as they believed that dynamic analysis could improve accuracy and performance. Every fragment is executed on Anubis and CWSandbox where actions of malware are identified. Analyzers generate results that use artificial intelligent and neural network depended on dynamic analysis. The malware are then grouped into malware families. Main disadvantage of the research is today's internet traffic which makes it impossible to use social analysis to achieve the desired results.

Another automatic behavior-based malware analysis framework was announced by Rieck et al. in [36] using machine learning. As most of the frameworks do, it collects many malicious samples and monitors their behavior using a sandbox virtual environment. After that conclusion and consideration, they inserted the results in a vector to implement and develop the algorithms. So, clustering was utilized to identify the families and clusters of malware with similar behavior. The classification was focused on attaching and connecting zero-day vulnerabilities to identified clusters. This was implemented to show and present the clustering and classification, focused and based on behavior-based analysis which can process the activities of malware executables every day.

Anderson et al. in [37] presented a malware detection algorithm based on the analysis of graphs constructed after the dynamic collection of instruction traces. Modification of malware analysis framework based on Ether was used to gather samples. Methodology suggests the control of 2-grams to state the likelihood of a Markov chain graph. System of graph kernels is implemented to compute and calculate similarity vector between instances in the learning phase. Two metrics that finds and searches similarities, a Gaussian kernel, which computes and calculates the local similarity between graph edges and a spectral kernel which computes the global similarity between charts, calculates a kernel vector. Critical dissimilar behaviors of malware determine the performance of various kernel learning procedures. A disadvantage is the high computational complexity, so the usage in actual situations and real environments is limited.

Bayer et al. in [38] suggested a method that puts effectively and automatically into classes, malicious datasets. In order to apply more information sources, an extension for Anubis was implemented with taint-propagation efficiencies. An abstraction of evidences was created in addition with an observable outline for every trail, which aids as input to the Locality Sensitive Hashing (LSH) algorithm. Researchers show the scalability of their method by classifying a large dataset of malware data in a few hours.

Tian et al. in [32] utilized an automated tool for extracting API call sequences from binaries while these are running in a virtual environment. Tian et al. utilized and applied classification methods from WEKA software to separate malicious data from good data but also, for classifying malware into their families.

Biley in [39] constructed a classifier that explains malware's activities regarding system changes. A firewall is used to restrict and protect from the impact of any sudden and unnecessary activity during examination. A behavioral identity of malicious behavior was developed which includes network connection and processes created. To perform connection of the malware samples, a distance metric known as normalized compression distance (NCD) was applied and tested. The method performed an automated categorization of a specific set of malware samples. Biley also measured and compared the fullness, integrity and condensation of the clusters and compared them with the clusters of AV vendors. As a disadvantage, it can be considered that analysts encountered problems with consistency as the efficiency and the status are static.

A malware classification method was suggested by Park et al. in [40] which depend on maximal component sub graph detection. First, a sandbox environment is used to execute and analyze malware samples, while system calls are taken, and a directed chart is created from these system call trays. For the comparison of the two programs the maximal common sub graph is calculated and estimated. However, there are some already known malware whose primary ability is to gain root authorization bypassing the analysis procedure.

Another procedure for malware detection proposed by Firdausi et al. in [41] analyzes malware samples using Anubis. Machine learning is used for processing information and records into sparse vector models for classification.

Nari & Ghorbani [42] developed a model for automatic malware classification into their specific and particular clusters depended on network performance. Their method depends on network traces applied as pcap input files to the model that have been analyzed, processed and extracted. Afterward, a graph and plot of the network activities of malware was presented. Some features of these figures are adopted and used to classify malware using classification algorithms.

Lee et al. has developed another machine learning method in [43] regarding clustering malicious software. After the dataset is performed in a virtual environment where reports are exported, a behavioral profile is produced which describes the sample's interaction with system resources. After the similarity between two profiles is computed, clustering algorithms are being applied like k-means and nearest neighbor to cluster them appropriately. In this method, the obstacle of obfuscation and execution-stalling techniques has made necessary the research of hybrid methods for better results.

Santos et al. in [44] again developed a hybrid zero-day detector called OPEM, which uses and exploits characteristics gathered and collected from the analysis of malevolent code. Signature-based malware analysis obtains the static characteristics, and dynamic malware analysis captures dynamic features. Two disparate datasets are compared through different classification algorithms. This method improves the accuracy and speed of both methods when running individually. Islam et al. [45] does something similar in [46].

Anderson et al. in [47] suggested a method, in which various information and features are utilized. Kernels based on Markov Chain graphs are being proposed for the binary file, disassembled file and two dynamic traces. A graph-let kernel is applied and implemented for the control flow graph. A Gaussian kernel is executed for the file information data matrix. In order to find weighted connections between the data multiple kernel learning is employed. Moreover, to categorize and separate the dataset into malicious and benign files, support vector machine classifier is applied. The results have shown great performance.

As literature shows data science proposes several solutions for categorizing malware. Machine Learning is increasingly being applied in a variety of industries. No doubt that Information Security should be one of those, as the extent and complexity of networks is ever increasing. Internet and "cloud" applications generate vast data sets from performance monitoring and event logs which require scalable and flexible techniques to distil useful and actionable information.

2.3 Cloud Computing

Cloud computing is an emerging technology paradigm that migrates current technological and computing concepts into utility-like solutions similar to electricity and water systems. Clouds bring out a wide range of benefits including configurable computing resources, economic savings, and service flexibility. However, security and privacy concerns are shown to be the primary obstacles to a wide adoption of clouds. The new concepts that clouds introduce, such as multi-tenancy, resource sharing and outsourcing, create new challenges to the security community. Addressing these challenges requires, in addition to the ability to cultivate and tune the security measures developed for traditional computing systems, proposing new security policies, models, and protocols to address the unique cloud security challenges. Khalil et al. [48] presented a comprehensive study of cloud computing security and privacy concerns. They identified cloud vulnerabilities, classified known security threats and attacks, and presented the state-of-the-art practices to control the vulnerabilities, neutralize the threats, and calibrate the attacks. Additionally, they investigated and identified the limitations of the current solutions and provide insights of the future security perspectives. Finally, they provided a cloud security framework in which they presented the various lines of defense and identified the dependency levels among them. Twenty eight cloud security threats were identified which were classified into five categories. Nine general cloud attacks along with various attack incidents, and provide effectiveness analysis of the proposed countermeasures were also presented.

Cloud computing environment has been extensively used for malware classification. Khorshed et al. present an extensive review on cloud computing with the main focus on gaps and security concerns [49]. They identified the top security threats and the existing solutions. They also investigated the challenges/obstacles in implementing threat remediation. To address these issues, they proposed a proactive threat detection model by adopting three main goals: (i) detect an attack when it happens, (ii) alert related parties (system admin, data owner) about the attack type and take combating action, and (iii) generate information on the type of attack by analyzing the pattern. Then some real cyber attacks were generated which can be detected from performance data in a hypervisor and its guest operating systems. They also employed modern machine learning techniques as the core of the model and accumulated a large database by considering the top threats. A variety of model performance measurement tools were applied to verify the model attack prediction capability.

One more model for malware detection on end hosts based on providing antivirus as an in-cloud network service has been proposed [50]. This model enables identification of malicious and unwanted software by multiple detection engines respectively. This approach provides several important benefits including better detection of malicious software, enhanced forensics capabilities and improved deployability. Malware detection in cloud computing includes a lightweight, cross-storage host agent and a network service. This model combines detection techniques, static signatures analyze and dynamic analysis detection. Using this mechanism it is found that cloud malware detection provides 35% better detection coverage against recent threats compared to a single antivirus engine and a 98% detection rate across the cloud environment.

2.4 Android malware detection

With the recent emergence of mobile platforms capable of executing increasingly complex software and the rising ubiquity of using mobile platforms in sensitive applications such as banking, there is a rising danger associated with malware targeted at mobile devices. The problem of detecting such malware presents unique challenges due to the limited resources available and limited privileges granted to the user, but also presents unique opportunity in the required metadata attached to each application. Shabtai et al. present a new behavior-based anomaly detection system for detecting meaningful deviations in a mobile application's network behavior [51]. The main goal of the android malware detection is to protect mobile device users and cellular infrastructure companies from malicious applications. More specifically, an attempt was made by [51] to detect a new type of mobile malware with self-updating capabilities that were recently found on the official Google Android marketplace. Malware of this type cannot be detected using the standard signatures approach or by applying regular static or dynamic analysis methods. The detection is performed based on the application's network traffic patterns only. The evaluation experiments by them demonstrate that: (1) various applications have specific network traffic patterns and certain application categories can be distinguished by their network patterns; (2) different levels of deviation from normal behavior can be detected accurately; (3) in the case of self-updating malware, original (benign) and infected versions of an application have different and distinguishable network traffic patterns that in most cases, can be detected within a few minutes after the malware is executed while presenting very low false alarms rate; and (4) local learning is feasible and has a low performance overhead on mobile devices.

Amos et al. present a machine learning based system for the detection of malware on Android devices [52]. Their system extracts a number of features and trains a One-Class Support Vector Machine in an offline (off-device) manner, in order to leverage the higher computing power of a server or cluster of servers. Sahs and Khan also studied the machine learning approach for android malware detection [53].

CHAPTER 3

IMPLEMENTATION

This chapter includes the details of datasets used, methodology, experiments performed and their performance.

3.1 Problem Description

The behavior of malicious software is studied to understand the security challenges, detect the malware behavior automatically using dynamic approach. The malwares are classified in this work and their performance is measured. The classifiers used in this research are k-Nearest Neighbors (kNN), J48 Decision Tree, and n-grams. The tests results were analyzed and the experiment results were compared.

3.2 System Requirements

Hardware Requirements

- System   : i7 – 2640M CPU, 2.80 GHz
- Hard disk   : 500 GB
- Monitor   : 1920 * 1080 Full HD
- Ram   : 8 GB
- Keyboard   : 110 keys enhanced

Software Requirements

- Operating system : Windows 7
- Front End   : Microsoft Visual Studio .Net 2010
- Adobe Flash player
- Java Jre 7
- .NET framework 4.0
- Adobe PDF reader

3.3 Datasets Used

The author utilized three datasets: A TrainLable, a test dataset, and a train dataset. The quantity of malware records and individually clean documents in these datasets appears in the initial two segments. As expressed over, the fundamental objective is to accomplish malware location with just a couple (if conceivable 0) of false positives, hence the spotless documents in this dataset (furthermore in the scale-up dataset) is much bigger than the quantity of malware records. The information set comprises of malware information set, both are in the arrangement of gathering (.asm) and byte (parallel).

From the entire list of capabilities that the author made for malware recognition, 308 double components were chosen for the investigations to be displayed in this work. Records that produce comparative qualities for the picked list of capabilities were checked just once. Note that the quantity of clean mixes i.e. blends of highlight qualities for the spotless documents in the three datasets is much little than the quantity of malware. These datasets mixes the spotless documents in the preparation of database which are mostly framework records (from distinctive forms of working frameworks) and executable and library records from diverse mainstream applications. The author likewise utilize clean records that are stuffed or have the same structure or the same geometrical likenesses with malware documents (e.g. utilize the same packer) keeping in mind the end goal to better prepare and test the framework.

The malware documents in the preparation dataset have been taken from the Training Data Set. The test dataset contains malware documents from the TrainLable accumulation and clean records from distinctive working frameworks (different documents that the ones utilized as a part of the first database). The malware accumulation in the preparation and test datasets comprises of Ramnit, Lollipop, Kelihos_ver3, Vundo, Simda, Tracur, Kelihos_ver1, Obfuscator-ACY and

Gatak sorts of malware. The primary and third sections speak to the rate of those malware sorts from the aggregate number of documents of the preparation and separately test data.

3.4 Process Outline

In this section the research plan is explained to be implemented in practice.

The whole process can be outlined in the following steps:

1. Sandbox configuration

2. Feature extraction

3. Feature selection

4. Application of the classification methods

5. Evaluation of the results

3.4.1 Sandbox Configuration

The Cuckoo Sandbox is configured to get the malware behavioral reports and to make sure that malware runs correctly with all of its functionality. In the real world different malware samples exploit different vulnerabilities that might be part of certain software products. Therefore, it is important to include a broad range of services in the virtual machines created by the sandbox. The hypervisor used for the virtual machines for Cuckoo is Virtualbox. The virtual machines will be created by using VMcloak, an automated virtual machine generation and cloaking tool for Cuckoo Sandbox [54].

3.4.2 Feature Extraction and selection

To solve the problem, the author had to extract relevant features from the dataset. This was the non-trivial part of the challenge to identify those features that would help to classify these files. Features are extracted from the reports generated by the sandbox.

Features used

1. The author started by taking the normalized frequency of the two digit hexadecimal values in the bytes file as the feature. Since each hexadecimal digit can take 16 values each, the author had 256 possible values and so a total of 256 feature in this case. The frequency of these 256 values was counted for each .bytes file in the dataset and normalized. A part of .bytes file of one of the malware is displayed in figure 5.

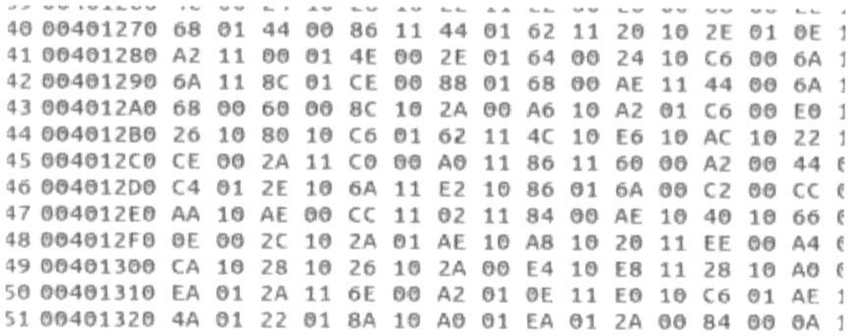

```
40 00401270 68 01 44 00 86 11 44 01 62 11 20 10 2E 01 0E 1
41 00401280 A2 11 00 01 4E 00 2E 01 64 00 24 10 C6 00 6A 1
42 00401290 6A 11 8C 01 CE 00 88 01 68 00 AE 11 44 00 6A 1
43 004012A0 68 00 60 00 8C 10 2A 00 A6 10 A2 01 C6 00 E0 1
44 004012B0 26 10 80 10 C6 01 62 11 4C 10 E6 10 AC 10 22 1
45 004012C0 CE 00 2A 11 C0 00 A0 11 86 11 60 00 A2 00 44 0
46 004012D0 C4 01 2E 10 6A 11 E2 10 86 01 6A 00 C2 00 CC 0
47 004012E0 AA 10 AE 00 CC 11 02 11 84 00 AE 10 40 10 66 0
48 004012F0 0E 00 2C 10 2A 01 AE 10 A8 10 20 11 EE 00 A4 0
49 00401300 CA 10 28 10 26 10 2A 00 E4 10 E8 11 28 10 A0 0
50 00401310 EA 01 2A 11 6E 00 A2 01 0E 11 E0 10 C6 01 AE 1
51 00401320 4A 01 22 01 8A 10 A0 01 EA 01 2A 00 84 00 0A 1
```

Figure 5. Screenshot of .bytes file

2. A similar feature was used for the .asm files, the only difference being that there were specific places in the .asm files, where the frequency was counted. In the given image, the author is counting the hex values in second column of each row (8C, 13, 31, 12, 94, etc.). A part of .asm file of one of the malware is displayed in figure 6.

```
.data:0044E8D7 8C              db    8Ch ; Œ
.data:0044E8D8 13              db    13h
.data:0044E8D9 31              db    31h ; 1
.data:0044E8DA 12              db    12h
.data:0044E8DB 94              db    94h ; "
.data:0044E8DC 11              db    11h
.data:0044E8DD CF              db    0CFh ; Ï
.data:0044E8DE 10              db    10h
.data:0044E8DF C8              db    0C8h ; È
.data:0044E8E0 13              db    13h
.data:0044E8E1 EA              db    0EAh ; ê
.data:0044E8E2 12              db    12h
.data:0044E8E3 B1              db    0B1h ; ±
.data:0044E8E4 11              db    11h
```

Figure 6. Screenshot of .asm file

3. Next, the author used the frequency of different assembly functions in the .asm files. The instructions used were like 'jump', 'push', 'pop', 'add', 'dec' and some others. Ten such functions were taken as the features.

4. The author also used other features like size of the files, Shannon entropy and a mixture of the above features. The author used the function of Shannon Entropy over the frequency of various bytes to get an idea of randomness of the files.

3.4.3 Application of classification methods

First of all n-gram algorithm was performed on the dataset. The test shows, the information set of 5231 malware tests with 9 classes from aggregate of 19118.

Algorithm: n-gram

---

malware<-read.csv("trainLabels.csv")

def join_ngrams (num = 100000):

dict_all = dict()

for c in range(1,10):

print "merging %i out of 9"%c

pickle.dump(dict_all, open('ready_for_selection.pkl','wb'))

load data

#instead of binary features, do count

  grams_dict = dict()

  for gram in grams_string:

    if gram not in grams_dict:

      grams_dict[gram] = 1

```
else:

    grams_dict[gram] += 1 binary_features = []
for feature in features_all:
    if feature in grams_dict:
        binary_features.append(grams_dict[feature])
    else: binary_features.append(0)
del grams_string'''
yield [f_id] + binary_features
```

with open('train_data_750.csv','wb') as outfile:

with open('test_data_750.csv','wb') as outfile:

"DONE 4 gram features!"

These specimens are subjectively parted into two bundles are arbitrarily parted into two parcels, a preparation and testing segment, preparing contains 2664 examples and test is 1332. The components like single-byte recurrence, byte 4 gram, direction check, capacity names and Derived Assembly Features (DAF) beat benchmark code in the gathering. For 4 gram bytes, the information addition is utilized to choose the best 500 elements for every class. For direction number, regular guidelines like "MOV" and "JMP" are tallied. Capacity name elements should be DLL highlights. It is replaced by social event just the capacity names rather for effortlessness. For DAF, every element is a standard representation of .asm directions, taking after the malware family: name. para1.para2, for example, or memory register. In the trial n-gram is picked and performed on the dataset. The Information Gain of every component was figured: $p(v\ C_j,)$

$IG\ j() = -vj\Sigma\ \Sigma \in (0,1)\ c \in \{cj\}\ P\ v\ C(j,)\log\ --p(vj\ )p(\ )\ C$

Where *IG j*( ) denote the Information Gain value of feature *j*, *C* represents one class in $\{C_i\}$, $\{C_i\}$ represent the class set of malware family. $p(v\ C_j,)$ denotes the probability of feature *j* with the value of v_j in class *C*. $p(v_j)$ denotes the probability of feature *j* equal v_j in all training sets. $p(\ )C$ denotes the probability of class *C* in all training sets. At last, the author will select features which have the lower *IG* value and save in the feature database.

3.5 Results and Discussion

To check the validity of the classifier, it is applied on the test set to get the probabilities of the malware file belonging to each of the 9 families. The prediction file, shown below in figure 7, gives a brief idea of this.

Feature	Score
256 hex values in bytes file(256 trees)	0.082228293
256 normalised hex values in bytes file(500 trees)	0.082421290
1st feature + size of the file	0.099343705
Shannon entropy	14.111708334
10 functions & 30 trees	0.140188703
Size of the files	5.610533917
14 functions & 10 trees	0.156611540
10 functions & 10 trees	0.153125351
256 hex values & 10 trees (.bytes)	0.192934515
256 hex values (.asm)	0.250228987

Figure 7. Screenshot of Prediction file

To evaluate the score in the competition is calculated using the multi-class logarithmic loss function, given by:

$$\log loss = -\frac{1}{N}\sum_{i=1}^{N}\sum_{j=1}^{M} y_{ij} \log(p_{ij})$$

The goal is to take the score as close to 0 as possible. The best score on the test board is 0.0.082228293, which uses the frequency of the 256 hex values as its features and uses random forest classifier. By using the other techniques, the following results were obtained:

ASM file Pixel Intensity Feature

Malwares can be visualized as grayscale images using the byte file. Each byte is from 0 to 255 so it can be easily translated into pixel intensity. However, it was found that image processing techniques doesn't work well with their features above. It was tried to extract a grayscale image from .asm file rather than the .byte file. This method is data driven and hence can't stop attack on same time.

Analysis

1. Frequency of hexadecimal values in the bytes file is actually equivalent to counting the frequency of the functions in the .asm files. The functions used in the malware make a lot of difference and so, it turned out to be a good feature.
2. Frequency of hexadecimal values at specific positions in the .asm file did not give a nice result. These values do not have any meaning related to them and were used because for the few files for which their frequency was checked, gave pretty good values.
3. Frequency of specific assembly language instructions. Some functions are more important than others. So, the same should be true for the viruses and hence, their frequency should have been a good feature but it turns out it is not.
4. The size of the files alone could not have been a very good feature, because the damage that a virus can cause is independent of its size. The function that a virus performs is mostly independent of its size and is verified by the results.

Based on the analysis of the tests and experimental results of all the 3 classifiers, the overall best performance was achieved by J48 decision tree with a recall of 96.3%. The accuracy of n-grams is 85.0% and KNN classifier shows an accuracy of 79.4%.

CHAPTER 4

CONCLUSION AND FUTURE WORK

In this chapter conclusion and the scope of future work is presented.

4.1 Conclusion

The essential target was to think about a machine learning design that insipidly perceives as much malware tests as it can. In the interim, the system is contrasted and compared with other methodology. Analysis demonstrates that the proposed strategy performs well. Malware identification by means of machine learning won't replace the standard discovery routines utilized by hostile to infection merchants, however will come as an expansion to them.

The execution examination of 3 unique classifiers was additionally, introduced. The general best execution was accomplished by J48 utilizing the term recurrence weight without highlight choice information set, with an exactness of 96.3%. The investigation of the tests revealed that the exploratory results presumed this evidence of idea is entirely powerful and effective in classifying malware.

4.2 Future Work

Although the dataset that was used in this study is broad, covering most of the malware types that are relevant to the modern world, it does not cover all possible types. Collecting a malware dataset is a tedious task that requires a lot of time and effort. For more accurate evaluation of the predictors, it is advised to test the models on all the possible types of malware: spyware, adware, rootkits, backdoor, banking malware, etc. In addition to that, it is important to understand that the model will only be able to predict the samples of the families that it has seen earlier. In other words, in a real-world application, the maximum amount of possible families should be used before using the present work for real-world environments.

References

[1] Kaspersky Labs. 2017. What is malware and how to defend against it? [Online]. Available at: http://usa.kaspersky.com/internet-securitycenter/internet-safety/what-is-malware-and-how-to-protect-against-it [Accessed 15 August 2017]

[2] Kaspersky Lab. 2016. Kaspersky Security Bulletin 2015. Overall statistics for 2015. [Online]. Available at: https://securelist.com/analysis/kaspersky-security-bulletin/73038/kaspersky-security-bulletin-2015-overall-statistics-for-2015/. [Accessed 15 August 2017]

[3] Juniper Research. 2016. Cybercrime will cost businesses over $2 trillion by 2019. [Online]. Available at: https://www.juniperresearch.com/press/press-releases/cybercrime-cost-businesses-over-2trillion. [Accessed on 15 August 2017]

[4] Fred Cohen. *Computer Viruses*. PhD thesis, University of Southern California, 1985.

[5] Horton, Jeffrey, and Jennifer Seberry. 1997. Computer Viruses. An Introduction. University of Wollongong.

[6] Smith, Craig, Ashraf Matrawy, Stanley Chow, and Bassem Abdelaziz. 2009. Computer Worms: Architectures, Evasion Strategies, and Detection Mechanisms. *Journal of Information Assurance and Security* 4.

[7] Dan Ellis. "Worm Anatomy and Model." In *Proceedings of the 2003 ACM workshop on Rapid malcode WORM '03*, pp. 42–50, 2003.

[8] Nicholas Weaver, Vern Paxson, Stuarts Staniford, and Robert Cunningham. "A Taxonomy of Computer Worms." In *Proceedings of the 2003 ACM workshop on Rapid malcode WORM '03*, pp. 11–18, 2003.

[9] Moffie, Micha, Winnie Cheng, David Kaeli, and Qin Zhao. 2006. Hunting Trojan Horses. *Proceedings of the 1st Workshop on Architectural and System Support for Improving Software Dependability*

[10] Chien, Eric. 2005. Techniques of Adware and Spyware. [Online] Available at: https://www.symantec.com/avcenter/reference/techniques.of.adware.and.spyware.pdf. [Accessed 15 August 2017]

[11] Chuvakin, Anton. 2003. An Overview of Unix Rootkits. *iDEFENCE Labs*

[12] Lopez, William, Humberto Guerra, Enio Pena, Erick Barrera, and Juan Sayol. 2013. Keyloggers. *Florida International University.*

[13] Savage, Kevin, Peter Coogan, and Hon Lau. 2015. The Evolution of Ransomware. Symantec Corporation. [Online]. Available at: http://www.symantec.com/content/en/us/enterprise/media/security_response/whitepapers/the-evolution-of-ransomware.pdf. [Accessed 15 August 2017]

[14] Thirumuruganathan, Saravanan. 2010. A Detailed Introduction to K-Nearest Neighbor (KNN) Algorithm. [Online]. Available at: https://saravananthirumuruganathan.wordpress.com/2010/05/17/A-detailed-introduction-to-k-nearest-neighbor-knn-algorithm/. [Accessed 15 August 2017]

[15] Laaksonen, Jorma, and Erkki Oja. 1996. Classification with learning k-Nearest Neighbors. In *Neural Networks, 1996., IEEE International Conference on* (Vol. 3, pp. 1480-1483). IEEE.

[16] Yiming Yang and Jan O. Pedersen. "A Comparative Study on Feature Selection in Text Categorization." In *Proceedings of the Fourteenth International Conference on Machine Learning*, pp. 412–420, 1997.

[17] Jeffrey O. Kephart and Bill Arnold. "Automatic Extraction of Computer Virus Signatures." In *Proceedings of the 4th Virus Bulletin Internation Conference*, pp. 178–184, 1994.

[18] Gerald J. Tesauro, Je_rey O. Kephart, and Gregory B. Sorkin. "Neural Network for Computer Virus Recognition." *IEEE Expert*, 11(4):5–6, 1996.

[19] William Arnold and Gerald Tesauro. "Automatically GeneratedWin32 Heuristic Virus Detection." In *Virus Bulletin Conference*, pp. 123–132, 2000.

[20] K.Wang W. Li and, S. Stolfo, , and B. Herzog. "Fileprints: Identifying File Types by n-gram Analysis." In *6th IEEE Information Assurance Workshop*, 2005.

[21] Matthew G. Schultz, Eleazar Eskin, Erez Zadok, and Salvatore J. Stolfo. "Data Mining Methods for Detection of New Malicious Executables." In *Proceedings of the IEEESymposium on Security and Privacy*, pp. 38–49, 2001.

[22] Matthew G. Schultz, Eleazar Eskin, Erez Zadok, Manasi Bhattacharyya, and Salvatore J. Stolfo. "MEF: Malicious Email Filter: A UNIX Mail Filter That Detects Malicious Windows Executables." pp. 245–252, 2001.

[23] Jeremy Z. Kolter and Marcus A. Maloof. "Learning to Detect Malicious Executables in the Wild."In *Proceedings of the 2004 ACM SIGKDD International Conference on Knowledge Discovery and Data Mining*, 2004.

[24] Tony Abou-Assaleh, Nick Cercone, Vlado Keselj, and Ray Sweidan. "N-Gram-Based Detection of New Malicious Code." In *Proceedings of the 28th Annual International Computer Software and Applications Conference - Workshops and Fast Abstracts - (COMPSAC'04) - Volume 02*, pp. 41–42, 2004.

[25] Tony Abou-Assaleh, Nick Cercone, Vlado Keselj, and Ray Sweidan. "Detection of new malicious code using n-grams signatures." In *Proceedings of Second Annual Conference on Privacy, Security and Trust*, pp. 193–196, 2004.

[26] InSeon Yoo. "Visualizing windows executable viruses using self-organizing maps." In *Proceedings of the 2004 ACM workshop on Visualization and data mining for computer security*, pp. 82–89, 2004.

[27] InSeon Yoo and Ulrich Ultes-Nitsche. "Non-Signature Based Virus Detection: Towards Establishing Unknown Virus Detection Technique Using SOM." *Journal in Computer Virology*, 2(3):163–186, 2006.

[28] Olivier Henchiri and Nathalie Japkowicz. "A Feature Selection and Evaluation Scheme for Computer Virus Detection." *icdm*, 0:891–895, 2006.

[29] Schultz, M. G., Eskin, E., Zadok, F., & Stolfo, S. J. (2001). Data mining methods for detection of new malicious executables. In *Proceedings 2001 IEEE Symposium on Security and Privacy. S P 2001* (pp. 38–49). https://doi.org/10.1109/SECPRI.2001.924286

[30] Kolter, J. Z., & Maloof, M. A. (2006). Learning to Detect and Classify Malicious Executables in the Wild. *J. Mach. Learn. Res.*, 7, 2721–2744.

[31] Kong, D., & Yan, G. (2013). Discriminant Malware Distance Learning on Structural Information for Automated Malware Classification. In *Proceedings of the 19th ACM SIGKDD International Conference on Knowledge Discovery and Data Mining* (pp. 1357–1365). New York, NY, USA: ACM. https://doi.org/10.1145/2487575.2488219

[32] Tian, R., Islam, R., Batten, L., & Versteeg, S. (2010). Differentiating malware from clean ware using behavioral analysis. *In 2010 5th International Conference on Malicious and Unwanted Software* (pp. 23-30).https://doi.org/10.1109/MALWARE.2010.5665796

[33] Santos, I., Devesa, J., Brezo, F., Nieves, J., & Bringas, P. G. (2013). OPEM: A Static-Dynamic Approach for Machine-Learning-Based Malware Detection. In Á. Herrero, V. Snášel, A. Abraham, I. Zelinka, B. Baruque, H. Quintián, E. Corchado (Eds.), *International Joint Conference CISIS'12-ICEUTE'12-SOCO'12 Special Sessions* (pp. 271–280). Springer Berlin Heidelberg. http://link.springer.com/chapter/10.1007/978-3-642-33018-6_28

[34] Siddiqui, M., Wang, M. C., & Lee, J. (2009). Detecting Internet worms using data mining techniques. *Journal of Systemics, Cybernetics, and Informatics*, 6(6), 48–53.

[35] Zolkipli, M. F., & Jantan, A. (2011). An approach for malware behavior identification and classification. In *2011 3rd International Conference on Computer Research and Development* (Vol. 1, pp. 191–194). https://doi.org/10.1109/ICCRD.2011.5764001

[36] Rieck, K., Trinius, P., Willems, C., & Holz, T. (2011). Automatic analysis of malware behavior using machine learning. *Journal of Computer Security*, 19(4), 639–668. https://doi.org/10.3233/JCS-2010-0410

[37] Anderson, B., Quist, D., Neil, J., Storlie, C., & Lane, T. (2011). Graph-based malware detection using dynamic analysis. *Journal in Computer Virology*, 7(4), 247–258. https://doi.org/10.1007/s11416-011-0152-x

[38] Bayer, U., Comparetti, P.M., Hlauschek, C. and Kruegel, C. (2009) Scalable, Be-havior-Based Malware Clustering. *Proceedings of the 16th Annual Network and Distributed System Security Symposium.*

[39] Biley. Worm Detection by Combination of Classification With Neural Networks Retrieved from http://www.iajet.org/iajet_files/vol.3/no.2/Worm Detection by Combination of Classification With Neural Networks.pdf

[40] Park, Y., Reeves, D., Mulukutla, V., and Sundaravel, B. (2010). Fast Malware Classification by Automated Behavioral Graph Matching. In *Proceedings of the Sixth Annual Workshop on Cyber Security and Information Intelligence Research* (p. 45). ACM. https://doi.org/10.1145/1852666.1852716

[41] Firdausi, I., Lim, C., Erwin, A., & Nugroho, A. S. (2010). Analysis of Machine Learning Techniques Used in Behavior-Based Malware Detection. *In 2010 Second In-ternational*

Conference on Advances in Computing, Control, and Telecommunication Technologies (pp. 201–203). https://doi.org/10.1109/ACT.2010.33

[42] Nari, S., & Ghorbani, A. A. (2013). Automated malware classification based on network behavior. In *2013 International Conference on Computing, Networking and Communications (ICNC)* (pp. 642–647). https://doi.org/10.1109/ICCNC.2013.6504162

[43] Lee, T., Mody, J., Lin, Y., Marinescu, A., & Polyakov, A. (2007, June 14). Application behavioral classification. Retrieved from http://www.google.com/pa-tents/US20070136455

Lee, T., and Mody, J.J. (2006) Behavioral Classification. *Proceedings of the European Institute for Computer Antivirus Research Conference* (EICAR'06)

[44] Santos, I., Nieves, J. and Bringas, P.G. (2011) Collective Classification for Unknown Malware Detection. *Proceedings of the International Conference on Security and Cryptography*, Seville, 18-21 July 2011, 251-256

[45] Islam, R., Tian, R., Batten, L. M., & Versteeg, S. (2013). Classification of malware based on integrated static and dynamic features. *Journal of Network and Computer Applications*, *36*(2), 646–656. https://doi.org/10.1016/j.jnca.2012.10.004

[46] Tian, R., Batten, L. and Versteeg, S. (2008) Function Length as a Tool for Malware Classification. *Proceedings of the 3rd International Conference on Malicious and Unwanted Software*, Fairfax, 7-8 October 2008, 57-64

[47] Anderson, B., Storlie, C. and Lane, T. (2012) Improving Malware Classification: Bridging the Static/Dynamic Gap. *Proceedings of 5th ACM Workshop on Security and Artificial Intelligence (AISec)*, 3-14

[48] Khalil, I.M., Khreishah, A. and Azeem, M., 2014. Cloud computing security: a survey. *Computers*, *3*(1), pp.1-35.

[49] Khorshed, M.T., Ali, A.S. and Wasimi, S.A., 2012. A survey on gaps, threat remediation challenges and some thoughts for proactive attack detection in cloud computing. *Future Generation computer systems*, *28*(6), pp.833-851.

[50] Hatem, S. S. and El-Khouly, M. M., 2014. Malware detection in Cloud computing. *International Journal of Advanced Computer Science and Applications (IJACSA)*, Vol. *5,No.4*.

[51] Shabtai, A., Tenenboim-Chekina, L., Mimran, D., Rokach, L., Shapira, B. and Elovici, Y., 2014. Mobile malware detection through analysis of deviations in application network behavior. *Computers & Security*, *43*, pp.1-18.

[52] Amos, B., Turner, H. and White, J., 2013, July. Applying machine learning classifiers to dynamic android malware detection at scale. In *Wireless communications and mobile computing conference (iwcmc), 2013 9th international* (pp. 1666-1671). IEEE.

[53] Sahs, J. and Khan, L., 2012, August. A machine learning approach to android malware detection. In *Intelligence and security informatics conference (eisic), 2012 european* (pp. 141-147). IEEE.

[54] C. Guarnieri, A. Tanasi, J. Bremer, and M. Schloesser, "Cuckoo's Sandbox," 2013. [Online]. Available: http://www.cuckoosandbox.org